This book is dedicated to Aline, William
"Bras de Fer" and Thomas Bjorn "Ironside"

In memory of Athos 2005 - 2016
'Gone but not forgotten'

The author of this book Benjamin James Baillie lives
and works in Normandy

THE PAGAN LORDS

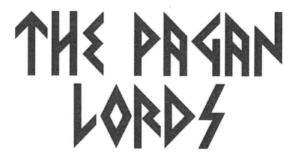

The forgotten Viking campaigns of the Great Heathen Army in France and Spain 840 – 982 AD

By Benjamin James Baillie

Contents

Introduction

The Viking age exploded like a thunderbolt out of the blue onto the international stage during the latter part of the 8th century. By the middle of the next century, the piratical raids for booty and plunder gave way to outright conquest and colonisation. In the West, the British Isles bore the brunt of this aggression in the form of the campaigns of the "Great Heathen Army" which not only dismantled the Anglo-Saxon Kingdoms of England, but also the Pictish and Briton dominions of modern day Scotland and the Celtic Principalities of Ireland. On the continent of mainland Europe Viking armies challenged the great Empire of Charlemagne. Ragnar Lodbrok's sack of Paris in 845 AD showed that no city or Kingdom was safe from the fury of the North-men. His sons and other Viking warlords embarked on a reign of terror that would bring Western civilisation to its very knees, eventually resulting in the creation of the Duchy of Normandy at the Treaty of St Clair Sur Epte in 911 AD. However Viking campaigns to create a second Normandy in Brittany, Aquitaine and Spain have been shrouded in mystery until now.

The Kingdom of Brittany (Breizh)

Brittany is situated on the far north western tip of modern day France, its coastline hugs the Atlantic Ocean in the west to the English Channel on its eastern border with Normandy. A bastion of Celtic culture, Brittany has a long tradition and links with the British Isles. The name Brittany actually means "Little Britannia" and this refers to the period  after the fall of the Roman Empire in the west when many of the Romano-British aristocracy fled their native homeland of Britain from the invading Angles, Saxons and Jutes and emigrated to Armorica (Roman name for Brittany). Indeed the legends and stories of King Arthur are deeply engrained in Breton culture and the areas in Brittany of Domnonée, Cornouaille and Léon were named after Devon, Cornwall and Caerleon. There may have also been a long standing Briton community already in Armorica before this migration. According to two Welsh sources, (The Dream of Maxen Wledic and the Historia Regum Britanniae) they recount that Conan Meriadoc (a Roman Commander) and his British-Romano legionaries were sent to Armorica by their General the usurper Magnus Maximus (self-proclaimed Roman Emperor) in the third century to press his claim in Gaul.

Historia Brittonum:

"The seventh Emperor was Maximus, He withdrew from Britannia with all its military forces, slew Gratianus the Emperor of the Romans, and obtained the sovereignty of all Europe. Unwilling to send back his warlike companions to their wives, families, and possessions in Britain, he conferred upon them numerous districts from the lake on the summit of Mons Lovis, to the city called Cant Guic, and to the Western Tumulus, that is Cruc Occident. These are the Armoric Britons, and they remain there to the present day. In consequence of their absence, Britain was overcome by foreign invaders; the lawful heirs were cast out, till God interposed with his assistance".

The newcomers intermixed with the local population and also the Alans, who were a fierce warrior race from the Russian steppe. They had been given land to settle by the last effective Roman commander in the west (Flavius Aetius) after the Battle of the Chalons in 451 AD. Together these different peoples became the Bretons and protected their freedom from the emerging Merovingian Empire of the Franks. By the 8th century Brittany became a thorn in the side of the new Frankish Carolingian dynasty. The Frankish hero Roland was made warden of the Breton March and ordered to shore up the frontier fortresses and check any Breton advances into Anjou and the Empire. After an internal insurrection by the Bretons amongst others from within the Carolingian Empire in 831 AD, the Emperor Louis I "the Pious" (Charlemagne's

Statue of Roland, Metz, France

son) installed a Breton nobleman by the name of Nominoe as Lord of Brittany. Nominoe remained a staunch ally of Louis I until the Emperor's death in 840 AD. Louis' death sparked a period of turmoil within the Empire, news of which filtered back to Scandinavia through the Viking trading networks. The Empire was split into three between Louis sons. Lothair I ruled over "Middle Frankia" from the imperial capital of Aachen, his brother Louis "the German" ruled over "Eastern Frankia" and Charles II "the Bold" controlled "Western Frankia" encompassing most of modern day France. The brothers fought each other in a civil war which lasted until the Treaty of Verdun in 843 AD.

During this period the Vikings took advantage of the confusion and launched their first organised raids deep into Carolingian territory.

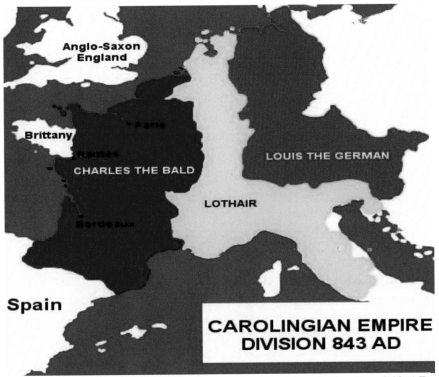

Map of the Carolingian Empire at the Treaty of Verdun 843 AD

In 841 AD a Viking raiding fleet under the command of the warlord Asgeir sailed up the river Seine and ransacked the rich abbeys of Juméges and Fontanelle (later renamed Saint Wandrille). The raiders even attacked the region's capital Rouen, burning it to the ground. Asgeir sailed back down the Seine and either over-wintered on Walcheren Island or on the safe haven of Noirmoutier, which had been used as a base since the departure of the monks from the Abbey of Saint Philbert in 835 AD.

These events also coincided with a change in Viking raiding tactics. The small individual raiding parties that had terrorised Western Europe for the last 50 or so years started to group together, forming huge fleets not just intend on raiding for plunder, but also to conquer and colonise the fertile lands of the British Isles and continental Europe.

The Ragnarsson Clan

One of the most prolific raiding groups of the ninth century was the Saekonungar (Sea Kings) of the Ragnarsson clan. The clan was led by one of the most fearsome adventurers of the day, Ragnar Lodbrok "Hairy breeches". In 845 AD he broke through the island defences of Paris and sacked the Frankish capital (see THE GREAT HEATHEN ARMY for more details). Ragnar had several sons, all with colourful names: Bjorn "Ironside", Hvitserk/Halfdan "the Wide embrace", Sigurd "Snake in the eye" Ivar "the Boneless", Ubba and Rognavald.

Ragnar's sons followed their father into a career of piracy and raiding. When according to the 'Ragnar Lodbrok Saga' Ragnar was killed in a pit of snakes by the Northumbrian King Ælla, Ivar "the Boneless" led his brothers in a vengeful campaign that saw the  destruction of the Anglo Saxon Kingdoms of East Anglia, Mercia, Northumbria and the Briton Kingdom of Strathclyde (modern day Scotland). Ivar eventually died peacefully in Ireland as King of Dublin. Halfdan and Ubba continued the conquest of England, but the last Kingdom 'Wessex' resisted and ultimately weathered the Viking onslaught under the leadership of King Æthelred and then Alfred. Haldan returned to the 'Danelaw' and became King of Jorvik (York). In 877 AD he was killed in Northern Ireland trying to press his claim as Ivar's heir apparent to the Kingdom of Dublin. Ubba returned to ravage Wessex and died fighting protecting his father's sacred raven banner 'guðfani' in the battle of Arx Cynuit (Devon). Bjorn "Ironside" gained fame as a pirate-adventurer, leading several raids against the Frankish Empire and eventually became King of Sweden. Sigurd also returned to Scandinavia and claimed the Danish crown.

RAGNAR "LODBROK"

The Battle of Messac/Blain, 843 AD

One of the first major targets of the Saekonungar was the ancient port city of Nantes (Condevincum). Nantes is situated on the mouth of the River Loire and was also the capital of the Breton March. The city was surrounded by a huge defensive wall constructed by the Romans in the 3rd century AD and was one of the most important cities in Western Frankia. At the battle of Fontenoy in 841 AD Ricwin the Count of Nantes died fighting for the Emperor Charles II "the Bold". Lambert (the previous Count's son) who had also fought for Charles at Fontenoy hoped that he would be made the next Count of Nantes, but Charles granted the title to Renaud d'Herbauges. Lambert was furious and raised an army in open revolt against Charles with troops from the garrisons of the Breton March. He sent word to Nominoe, who decided that the time was right to rise up and throw off the Frankish yoke and push for full independence for Brittany. Renaud d'Herbauges spies brought back word that a Breton force under the command of Nominoe's son, Eprisoe was in the vicinity of Messac (near Rennes) and had not yet joined forces with Lambert. Renaud decided to launch a pre-emptive strike against the rebels and marched towards Messac. As the Breton forces crossed the river Vilaine, Renaud launched a surprise attack and routed the advanced guard. At this very moment Lambert arrived on the field of battle and charged into the fray. Now attacked from both sides Renaud and his men were slaughtered. According to the Chronicle of Nantes, Renaud was killed at Blain, some 45 kms south of Messac on the banks of the river L'Isac. After his initial victory at Messac he was killed in a surprise attack by the combined forces of Eprisoe and Lambert on his return to Nantes. Whichever version is correct the outcome remains the same and Lambert entered Nantes triumphant and proclaimed himself Count. After only a few weeks it seems the citizens of Nantes tried to depose Count Lambert and threw him out of the city.

The Sack of Nantes 24th June 843 AD

The events on the Breton March had been closely followed by a Viking fleet anchored on the island of Noirmoutier. Although the sources give no mention of who commanded this fleet, it was probably led by either Asgeir, who had raided the Seine valley only two years before or by the formidable warlord Hastein, who was a close colleague/relation of Ragnar Lodbrok "Hairy breaches". Hastein had been active along the coastline in Northern France conducting raids, including an attack on Coutances Cathedral (Cotentin, Normandy) in 836 AD.

According to the Annals of Angers, Count Lambert in league with the Vikings devised a plan to re-capture Nantes and punish its disloyal burgers and citizens.

Annals d'Angers;

"Lambert was impious and traitorous; he led the pagan ships up the river Loire to Nantes and sacked the city"

Carefully choosing the holy day of Saint John (24th of June), the Vikings used the cover of the celebrations of the Baptist's feast to launch the attack on the city. With the help of Count Lambert Hastein's ships navigated the Loire estuary avoiding the sandbanks, treacherous marshes and advanced unsuspectingly towards Nantes. As the inhabitants of the city revelled, dancing, singing and praying the Viking marauders scaled the city walls using makeshift ladders and ropes. According to the "Miracles of St Martin de Vertou" another contingent entered to city posing as merchants, hiding their weapons under their clothes. Once inside they revealed their true identity and went on the rampage. The garrison of Nantes had been stripped bare during the recent struggle between Count Renaud and Count Lambert and could offer little resistance against the invaders. The celebrations turned into a bloodbath as the Vikings rampaged through the tightly packed streets, hacking down all who stood in their way. The carnage was horrendous, men women and children were slaughtered like lambs by the blood thirsty North-men.

Histoire de Bretagne 1588, written from an eyewitness source;

"Children hanging on their dead mothers' breasts drank blood rather than milk. The stone flags of the church were spattered with the blood of the clergymen and the holy alter dripped with the blood of the innocent. The pagans then pillaged the entire city, taking all its treasures and set fire to the church"

Bishop Gohardus and the leading clergy retreated to the safely of the church of St Peter and Paul and barred the great wooden doors, hoping that they would stop the pagans from entered god's sacred ground. It was to no avail as Viking berserkers relentlessly hacked through the doors and massacred the Bishop and his flock. Gohardus cried out "Sursum Corda" (lift up your ears to God) before his was finished off by a Viking battle axe.

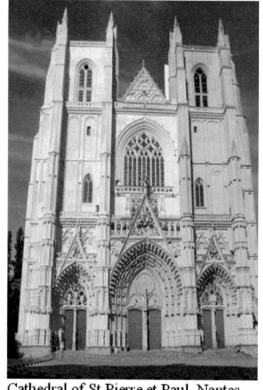

Cathedral of St Pierre et Paul, Nantes

As nightfall descended, Hastein's Vikings returned back to their ships laden down with an enormous amount of gold, silver and slaves. They sailed back to the island of Noirmoutier from where they planned their next course of action. Many of the captives were ransomed back to those who had hidden their wealth during the attack. The unfortunate others who could not afford the ransom were sold off into a lifetime of slavery. On the 29th of June only 5 days after the attack on Nantes Hastein sent another raiding party back up the Loire to attack the rich abbey at Indre. After stripping it of its gold and silver platter the pagans destroyed the abbey and burned it to the ground.

The great raid on Aquitaine and Spain 843-844 AD

After the devastating sack of Nantes, the Vikings launched another daring raid on the Garonne River in the province of Aquitaine. Stretching from the Pyrenees Mountains in the south to the Breton border in the north, Aquitaine was one of the greatest Duchies in

France. Situated 160 km south of their island refuge of Noirmoutier, the river Garonne connects Aquitaine's ancient cities of Bordeaux, Agen and Toulouse just outside the province's eastern frontier. Bordeaux had briefly been raided in 840 AD, but its huge Roman walls had been reinforced and posed a formidable obstacle to any would-be attacker. According to the Annals of St Bertin the Vikings by passed Bordeaux and raided the unprotected communities of the Garonne. Their ultimate target was the prosperous city of Toulouse. Although Toulouse is located over 300 km from the Atlantic coast the Viking longships were able to penetrate the river Garonne inland due their shallow hulls. Toulouse befell the same fate as Nantes and was ransacked by the Pagans.

Annals of St Bertin;

"The Nordomanni (Vikings) sailed up the Garonne as far as Toulouse wreaking destruction everywhere, without encountering any opposition. Some of them withdrew and sailed south to Galicia where they were defeated by stone throwing machines. The remnants of the raiding party sailed on further south and attacked the Saracens of the South Western part of the Iberian peninsular."

Aerial view of the island of Noirmoutier, France

On returning to the Garonne estuary the Viking fleet separated. Half of it returned back to the island of Noirmoutier, while the remainder sailed on south towards Spain. Hugging the coastline away from the stormy waters of the Bay of Biscay they passed into Spanish waters. On the 1st of August 844 AD the fleet anchored at Gijon which is one of the only safe harbours on the Cantabrian coast. It is not recorded that Gijon was sacked, but anything outside the Roman defensive walls would probably have been plundered. Once the landing party had gathered supplies and reconnoitered the area they set sail west towards Galicia.

The Chronicle Rotense
"People hitherto unknown, pagan and very cruel"

The Spanish region of Galicia offered the Vikings many safe havens from the unpredictable Atlantic weather, such as the Gulf of Ártabro which is formed by four estuaries: A Coruña, Betanzos, Ares and Ferrol. As the fleet entered the mouth of the Gulf of Ártabro they caught sight of the Torre de Hércules. This was an ancient Roman lighthouse built in the reign of the Emperor Trajan (1st century AD). Disembarking near the old Roman port of Ptolomeus Flavium Brigantium the Vikings ransacked the settlement and wasted the land.

The Tower of Hercules (Farum Brigantium) Galicia

As they collected their plunder from the surrounding vicinity they were surprised by the arrival of the Asturian defence force comprised of Counts and Dukes sent by King Ramiro to check the Viking invasion. Faced against an organised army the Vikings fought a fighting retreat back to their ships.

In the melee several Viking longships were burnt and sunk by the advancing Asturians. After this partial defeat the Viking fleet regrouped and headed south towards Moorish Spain instead of returning home empty handed. If the Vikings measured their raids in plunder then the raid south had so far been unfruitful.

As the drakkars crossed over into Al-Andalus waters they made their first recorded contact with the Moors of the Arab world. Like a thunderbolt out of the blue, the city of Lisbon was caught by surprise and sacked by the heathens.

The arrival of the Vikings caused a panic amongst the inhabitants of the region who fled into the mountains to seek refuge. Lisbon's governor, Wahballah Hazm sent an urgent letter to the Emir of the desperate situation he faced and informed him that 54 Viking ships and a number of smaller vessels had landed in force. Using the famous Gokstad ship discovered in Vestfold, Norway as an indicator, the Viking force may have numbered some 2,000-2,500 warriors.

The Moorish Chronicler Ahmad B Muhammad Arrazi;

"Towards the end of 844 AD there appeared the ships of the Northmen – known in Alandalús as magicians "Madjus" on the Western coast of Alandalús, and on the first Wednesday of the month they stopped in Lisbon, taking the city as the gate to what then seemed a game reserve. They stayed there for thirteen days, in which they were involved in three battles with the local Moors".

The Emir sent out letters to the governors of the coastal towns for them to be alert, but by the time this information reached them the "Madjus" had already struck again. This time Cadiz and then Sedona were next to fall to the dreaded sack. Like the Christians of the white Christ the Vikings had no respect for the holy places of the Prophet Mohammad, stripping them of their wealth and holy treasures.

The Madjus was the nickname which the Moors gave to the Vikings. It means magicians which may refer to the Vikings ability to strike quickly, using extreme surprise and aggression. The key to the Viking raids was their ships which were stealthy and very versatile, whether in the open sea or in the shallowest of rivers. Using their longships and tactics developed over the last 50 years they caused havoc against the Moors, who were simply not prepared to combat this new sea menace.

Using the river Guadalquivir, part of the fleet advanced inland towards Seville. Abandoning the city, the garrison fled and established a rallying point at Carmona.

The Emir of Cordoba

The Vikings looted Seville and sent out word for the rest of the fleet to join them there. For over a week they captured, killed and terrorised the city's inhabitants. The Emir Abd ar-Rahman II advanced from Córdoba with a large cavalry force and was joined by the local militias at Cordova. Meanwhile unaware of the force amassing against them, the Vikings sent out some raiding parties towards Constantina, Fuete de Cantos, Cordova and Moron.

At Quirtas de Moafer south of Seville they were enticed into giving battle and ambushed by the Emir's force. Realising that a large army of Moorish troops were advancing on Seville, the Viking leaders tried to recall the raiding parties, but it was too late. The Emir's men overran Seville's makeshift defences and besieged some of the Vikings in the citadel. Caught by surprise the cohesion of the Viking fleet quickly disintegrated. Over thirty longships were destroyed and burnt at Tejada.

In Ibn Hayyan

"The bloodiest battle against them took place on Wednesday near Seville in the parish of Tlyatah (Tejada). In this fight many died and were annihilated by God: thirty of their boats burnt, many of their dead hung on posts, and others were tied to the trunks of the Seville palm trees. From the moment in which they entered Seville beating the locals, until the day in which they were beaten and finally left the city, forty days lapsed"

One group of Vikings managed to escape the carnage and get back to their ships, picking up some survivors from the ambush at Quirtas de Moafer. As they made their way downstream they were harassed from both sides of the riverbank by the Emir's troops and the local population who threw stones and animal bones at them.

In a last desperate attempt to salvage something from the raid, one of the Viking leaders ransomed back some of the captives for food and clothing. This may indicate the pitiful state of what was left of the once mighty raiding fleet. The unfortunate Vikings that were not able to escape were brutally punished and executed. Some 200 decapitated heads were even sent over North Africa as a present for the Berber Emirs. So ended the first great recorded raid on the Iberian Peninsula, the Christian and Muslim Kingdoms of Spain had defeated the "Madjus" after a bloody reign of terror, but the invaders would return in even greater numbers.

Frankia, further attacks and internal revolts
844-846 AD

In November 844 AD King Charles II arrived on the Breton March in person to try and compel Nominoe and Count Lambert into submission. The King pushed as far as Rennes, but was unable to bring the rebels to battle. When Charles headed south into Aquitaine to besiege Toulouse, the Breton and rebel forces crossed over the border and raided deep into Anjou and Maine. Nominoe was forced to return home when news reached him of a series of raids by the Vikings on the Breton coastline. In October an imperial synod was convened at Yutz in Eastern Frankia. High ranking Bishops were dispatched to Nominoe, Count Lambert and Pepin II 'the King of Aquitaine' to offer the King's peace or face total war. Both Count Lambert and Pepin accepted, but Nominoe refused and carried on the struggle for Breton independence.

He may have been confident that Charles would not be able to attack him after his humiliating defeat by Rangar Lodbrok's victory over the Frankish forces near the River Seine and the sack of Paris.

The sack of the capital was not the only disaster to befall the Empire in 845 AD. In Aquitaine the Vikings returned and sacked Angouléme, Perigord and the ancient town of Saintes. The local Frankish militia led by Séguin (Count of Gascogne) fought bravely against the invaders, but was overwhelmed and slaughtered. The Count refused to flee and was killed in the melee.

The Vikings returned to their ships laden down with the spoils from the raid, leaving Saintes a smoldering heap of ruins, only the Roman arch of Germanicus was left standing.

L'Arc de Germanicus. Saintes. France

By the winter of 845 AD Charles was ready to take the war to Brittany. With the help of some Breton defectors he marched against Nominoe at the head of a huge host. On the 22nd of November just north of Redon near the Abbey of Ballon the Frankish forces formed into battle formation and advanced towards the Breton positions on the other side of the boggy field. Using the local knowledge of the wetland terrain, Nominoe lured the King's men deeper into the marshes. Unable to use their heavy cavalry in the boggy ground the Frankish forces were easy prey for the lightly armoured Breton skirmishers. With heavy loses Charles called off the attack and retreated back to Le Mans where he regrouped. The campaign of 846 AD ended with a negotiated agreement, though the exact details are unknown. Nominoe was forced onto the defensive when the Loire based Vikings raided deep into Brittany. St Bertin reported that the Bretons were defeated in three battles. Nominoe fled and later bought off the Vikings with the Danegeld.

The siege of Bordeaux 848 AD

Ragnar's sack of Paris in 845 AD, the destruction of Saintes and the internal revolts within the Western Empire had exposed the weakness of King Charles II ability to exercise control over the large swaves of land from the foothills of the Pyrenees to the river Rhine. The Vikings were fully aware they had the advantage of surprise and that they could strike at the very heart of the Empire using the great inland rivers of the Seine, Loire, Garonne and Saône. The 340 Km infiltration of the river Garonne during the great raid of 843 AD had proved this point perfectly.

Politics in Aquitaine led to the Vikings launching another great campaign south in late 847 AD. A huge Viking fleet gathered at Noirmoutier for an audacious attack on the capital of Aquitaine itself: Bordeaux. The nominal leader of the fleet was Asgeir, the same Viking warlord who had attacked the Seine valley in 841 AD. This time the Viking strategy was not just a seasonal raid, but nothing other than to capture and conquer Aquitaine. Bordeaux was the greatest city south of the Loire and a commercial centre strategically positioned on the crossroads between the Atlantic Ocean, the Mediterranean Sea and the Iberian Peninsula.

This lucrative trade route was certainly an important target for the Vikings who were starting to create a piecemeal trading Empire from the Fjords of Norway to the newly established Longport's in Ireland.

Sketch showing Bordeaux's Roman/Medieval ramparts

Bordeaux had thwarted two separate Viking raids, 840 and 843 AD partly because it was protected by a huge series of 9 meter Roman walls, but the fleet which rowed up the Garonne River was determined to capture the city at all costs. Asgeir's Vikings besieged the city and captured all the surrounding villages and towns, tightening the noose around Bordeaux.

When King Charles II heard the news of Bordeaux's plight he raised a feudal army and marched south. By Easter 848 AD he had arrived at the halfway point in Poitiers. When his spies brought back word that part of the Viking army attacking Bordeaux was encamped on the banks of the River Dordogne he marched on and destroyed this force, capturing nine Viking longships in the process.

Pippin II (the King of Aquitaine) made no attempt to relieve the city and sometime in late 848 AD Bordeaux fell to Asgeir's Vikings. According to the Annals of St Bertin the Jews betrayed the city to the Vikings.

"In Aquitaine some Jews betrayed Bordeaux to the Danes, having taken the city, they ravaged and burned it."

The fall of Bordeaux signaled the end for the inactive Pippin II who was deposed by his own people. King Charles II forces were not strong enough to retake Bordeaux from the Vikings and he retired to Orleans where he was symbolically crowned King of Aquitaine. In 849 AD Asgeir furthered his control over the region by launching a devastating attack on the city of Périgueux. In 851 AD Nominoe of Brittany died whilst ravaging Carolingian territory near Vendôme. His son Eprisoe continued the war against Charles, defeating him at the Battle of Jengland. This important battle led to the Treaty of Angers in which Brittany gained its independence. Eprisoe gained the title of King, but remained a vassal of King Charles II although with much greater autonomy than ever before. The restoration of Franco-Breton relations allowed both leaders to turn their attention to combat the Viking menace.

Campaign on the Seine 851-856 AD

In 851 AD Asgeir left Bordeaux and sailed north around the Cape of Finistère (Brittany) into his old stomping ground of the Seine estuary. It had been ten years since his first raid on the Seine valley. Asgeir may have launched his attack in the north to lure away any Frankish campaigns on the fledgling Viking colony in Aquitaine. It is equally possible he was trying to accrue as much treasure and prestige as possible in a bid to gain the Danish crown. Denmark had been in the midst of a civil since King Horik I had executed some of the followers of Ragnar Lodbrok.

In 850 AD his own nephews had made an attempt upon his life and many other warlords at home and abroad were baying for the crown.

Using the high estuary tide, Asgeir's fleet arrived at the Abbey of Fontenelle (St Wandrillle) on the 13th of October by complete surprise. This time he ransacked the abbey, stripping it of its treasures and murdered some of the hapless monks. For 89 days his forces fanned out over the area raiding and plundering everything in their wake. He returned to Fontenelle on January 9th 852 AD and possibly after not receiving anymore tribute from the surviving clergy he had the abbey burned to the ground.

The city of Rouen was next to feel the wrath of the Viking warlord and was plundered. Asgeir set up a fortified position in the smoldering ruins of the Cathedral to be used as a base to further terrorise the region. He then decided on a risky overland raid deep into Frankish territory far away from the safety of his longships stationed on the river Seine. His target was the rich town of Beauvais, some 80km on foot from Rouen. Asgeir's men marched quickly along the ancient Roman road through the Forest of Lyons to increase the speed and surprise of the attack on Beauvais. The town was taken be complete surprise and ransacked in a steer act of violent brutality. Overconfident, the Viking raiding force took a small detour to attack the Abbey of Saint-Germer-de-Fly just south of Gournay en Bray on their return journey.

This was a tactical error as they had lost the element of surprise and were deep in enemy territory. News of the sack of Beauvais had reached to court of King Charles II who at once sent a large mounted force to check the Viking raid. Obtaining information from fleeing refugees, the Frankish defence force was able to pinpoint the Viking position and catch up with the raiders at the modern day village of Vardes. Charging out from all directions the Frankish cavalrymen slaughtered the heavily laden down Vikings with vicious zeal.

ASGEIR

Some survivors managed the make their way back to Rouen through the Forest of Lyons, while others followed the small streams and rivers that led back to the Seine.

Asgeir was one of the lucky survivors and managed to regroup the remnants to his army back in Rouen. He decided to abandon the city and find a more defensive position to over winter. The islands of Jeufosse (between Vernon and Bonnières) and Oissel were chosen. From these islands Asgeir knew it would be near impossible for King Charles II forces to attack him.

The Abbey of Saint Germer de Fly attacked in Asgeir's raid

By the early summer of 853 AD Asgeir left his island bases and returned back down the river Seine towards the coast. The rest bite did not last long for the Franks, as Asgeir's Vikings were replaced by another huge raiding fleet under the command of Godfrid Haraldsson.

Godfrid Haraldson "The scourge of the North"

Godfrid was the son of the Danish King (Harald Klak 812-814 and again 819-827 AD). He had actually been baptised by Lothair I (King of Middle Frankia) and Charles' II brother. Although Godfrid had served the King loyally in the early 850s AD, he defected and joined forces with his cousin Rorik in an attack on the Middle Empire.

Their objective was to carve out a Viking Kingdom in Frisia (modern day Holland). Frisia was devastated and in the end Lothair I had no choice but to cede the important trading port of Dorestad on the mouth of the River Rhine to Godfrid and Rorik's Vikings.

After capturing Dorestad Godfrid sailed south into the English Channel. On the 9th of October 853 AD he arrived in the Seine estuary and sailed up the river towards Rouen. A Frankish naval force caught sight of the advancing Viking Drakkars and decided to confront the invaders. Somewhere on the river between the old Roman port of Aizier and the Abbey of Fontenelle (St Wandrille) a vicious naval battle took place. Using to high tide Godfrid was able to use the speed and maneuverability of his ships to quickly overwhelm the Frankish vessels. Viking berserkers clambered aboard the burning Frankish ships and finished off the survivors, throwing the bodies overboard into the bloody waters of the Seine.

River Seine at Aizier, location of the 9th century naval battle

As the fleet continued upstream, King Charles II requested help from his brother Lothair I. The two Kings marched together at the head of a vast army towards Rouen, intend on destroying the Viking raiders.

Godfrid's assault was checked and he was forced to over winter his fleet on the island of Oissel with the Frankish army arrayed on both sides of the river Seine hemming him in. A stalemate ensued, Godfrid was unwilling to attack the Franks and they intern did not have the capability to launch an amphibious attack on the island.

In the spring, Godfrid slipped away and sailed around the Breton coast to Noirmoutier. Seeking easier prey he launched an attack on the Loire estuary, Nantes was sacked for the second time and Godfrid decided to continue upstream sacking all the settlements in his wake.

The great city of Tours, some 200 kms inland was razed to the ground in an audacious attack. Only the quick thinking of the monks managed to save the holy relics of St Martin which were taken to the safety of the Abbey of Cormery. Resistance hardened when Bishop Agius and Bishop Burchard raised the feudal forces of Orleans and Chartres, blocking any further raiding inland.

As Godfrid's Vikings returned down the Loire another Viking fleet appeared off the Breton coastline. The Breton Duke Eprisoe, fearing that Brittany would be the next target if these

King Charles II "the bald"

two fleets joined forces entered into negotiations with the newly arrived Vikings under Sigtrygg. The Viking warlord agreed to join the Bretons and together they attacked Godfrid's Vikings on the island of Île de Grande Biesse, just outside Nantes. The attack was beaten back and Godfrid's men slaughtered the Viking-Breton force. During the night, Sigtrygg sent a messenger to Godfrid and proposed an alliance, thus betraying the Bretons.

As the morning mist dispersed, Godfrid's fleet of 130 longships sailed past Sigtrygg's fleet unmolested. Duke Eprisoe had been double crossed, but he could do nothing to stop Godfrid's fleet from sailing up the river Redon into the heart of Brittany. Only a violent storm stopped the Vikings from destroying the whole of Southern Brittany. They did however capture the Bishop of Vannes in the ravaging of the region. He was eventually ransomed back in return for a large amount of money. Brittany was saved from further Viking aggression for the time being when news reached Godfrid that King Horik had been murdered in Denmark. He returned to Dorestad where he joined Rorik in a joint venture to capture the Danish crown.

Bjorn "Ironside" Ragnar Lodbrok's son

In 856 AD Viking active in Frankia intensified, While King Charles II was trying to establish his authority in Aquitaine, the Vikings launched and two pronged attack on the Carolingian heart lands. Bjorn "Ironside" the son of the legendary Viking Ragnar "Lodbrok" led an enormous Viking fleet into the Seine estuary. He was followed by a second fleet under Sigtrygg from the Loire. Together they lay laid waste to every settlement all the way from the coast to Pitres in the Vexin region near to Paris. Using the island of Jeufosse they prepared for the greatest prize of all: Paris. Meanwhile a third fleet simultaneously sailed into the Loire. This fleet was probably commanded by Ragnar's old right hand man Hastein who had been using the Channel Islands to strike at the Breton and Neustrian coastline. Hastein's raiders struck deep inland and even launched an attack on Blois.

Bjorn followed in his father's footsteps and sacked Paris, only the Abbeys of Saint Denis, Saint Germain des Prés, Saint Stephen and Saint Vincent were spared because of their payment of 'Danegeld' to Bjorn's marauding Vikings. Charles II returned north and managed to drive the Vikings back from an abortive raid near Chartres to their winter base on Oissel Island. Then in the dark depths of winter (January, 857 AD) Bjorn felt strong enough to launch a surprise revenge attack on Chartres. This time Bjorn's men broke through the city's defences and went berserk, massacring the population including Bishop Frotbald. The fall of Chartres sent shockwaves through North Western Frankia and resistance crumbled in the face of the Viking onslaught. Evreux was plundered and Charles II lost effective control in Neustria. In 858 AD Bjorn was joined by Hastein and together they attacked the Parisian abbeys that had been untouched during the 856 AD raid.

William de Jumièges describing Bjorn and Hastein's attack on Frankia:
"Ships are built, shields repaired, armour and helmets polished, swords and spears sharpened; the army is carefully supplied with weapons. Then on the appointed day the ships are dragged down to the sea. Sailors aboard in earnest, banners are raised, sails flutter in the wind and the wolves sail off to mangle the Lord's sheep, offering their god Thor a taste of human blood".

Unable to defeat the combined forces of Bjorn and Hastein, Charles II bribed the warlords at Verberie to leave his territory. Charles may have even offered them the fief of Chartres, which was sold by Hastein to a Frankish Count for 500 cows. With the departure of Bjorn and Hastein, Sigtrygg took command of the remaining Seine Vikings and forced Charles to pay a huge ransom for the Abbot of Saint Denis, who had been captured near Paris. The following year Sigtrygg raided the Northern bank of the Seine, ransacking Noyon, Laon and Beauvais.

Charles' inability to defend his Kingdom led to several of his nobles reengaging their oaths of allegiance. Stripped of manpower, the King was forced to pay one Viking warlord to attack another. When a new Viking fleet appeared in the Somme estuary Charles sent envoys to their leader Weland. The King offered him 3000 pounds of gold and provisions of food and wine if he would clear the Seine of Sigtrygg's Vikings once and for all.

Weland agreed and when his main force returned from raiding the Wessex coast (England) he sailed into the Seine estuary and besieged his fellow compatriots on the island of Oissel. Sigtrygg, trapped like a rat offered Weland a counter offer of 6000 pounds of silver. Weland double crossed King Charles II and allowed Sigtrygg and his fleet to abandon their island base unmolested and sail out to the open sea.

Weland continued up the Seine and made a fortified base for himself at Melun just outside the capital (Paris). To strengthen his grip around Paris he dispatched his son to secure and fortify the monastery of Meur des Fosses. By doing this he was able the control river traffic on both the Seine and Marne rivers. When part of Weland's fleet was seen advancing east towards Meaux, Charles II was galvanised into action. He immediately ordered the construction of fortified bridges along the Seine and Marne around Paris. These measures effectively trapped Weland and his men. When the Meaux contingent tried to re-unit with their compatriots at Meur des Fosses they were shocked to find that the river Marne was blockaded at Trilbardou (Lagny). Unable to leave the safety of their ships Weland and his fleet submitted to King Charles II. The defeat was decisive and Weland's fleet disbanded almost immediately. The King encouraged some to them to join his army and even Weland himself agreed to be baptised. The remainder of the fleet spilt up and sailed down the Seine, stopping at the Viking shipyard at

Jumièges to repair their ships before finally sailing on to join the
Loire Vikings or return home to Scandinavia.

Bjorn and Hastein's great raid south

With the "Danegeld" obtained from King Charles II, Bjorn and
Hastein headed south to Noirmoutier Island where they planned one
of the greatest raids of the Viking age. After recruiting a fleet of 62
ships (2000-3000 fighting men) the warlords set out towards Spain
and the unknown. Indeed they had inside knowledge and may have
even had some sailors aboard from the original raid some twenty
years earlier. Following the same route as the 844 AD raid Bjorn
and Hastein's fleet hugged the Spanish coast, briefly landing in
Galicia. There they plundered the Arousa estuary, before being
forced to leave when Earl Pedro arrived with the Galician defence
force. With the element of surprise lost in Galicia, the fleet headed
south, raiding around the Gulf of Cadiz, near Seville. Both the
Christian and Muslim Kingdoms of modern day Spain and Portugal
had bolstered up their defences since 844 AD, which made raiding
extremely hazardous.

Bjorn "Ironside" and Hastein's Mediterranean raid 859-862 AD

After sacking the port of Algeciras (Spain) the Vikings slipped through the straits of Gibraltar and landed in force in the Maghreb Al-Aqsa Emirate of Northern Morocco. The town of Nekor was taken by surprise and ransacked

"The Madjus, God curse them landed at Nekor and plundered it and made its inhabitants slaves"

The Emir sent a hastily gathered Moorish defence force to drive the invaders back into the sea, but they were slaughtered by Bjorn and Hastein's men in a vicious encounter outside the gates of Nekor.

According to the Irish annals the King of Mauretania fought against the sons of Ragnar Lodbrok and was defeated, losing his hand in the battle. With no one to stop them, the Vikings looted the homes and buildings of Nekor. For 8 days they devastated the area before returning to their ships laden down with booty and slaves. The Northmen also captured several African slaves called 'blámenn', (blue men) in Norse. These unfortunate soles ended up in the slave market in Dublin, possibly taken to Bjorn's brother Ivar 'the Boneless' who was the co-ruler of the Viking colony along with Olaf the White.

The ruins of Orihuela castle used by the Vikings as a winter base

Bjorn was still hungry for more adventure and instead of returning home the fleet continued up the Eastern coast of Spain destroying almost all the settlements in their wake. In the Valencia region Bjorn's Vikings infiltrated the Seguera River and captured the town of Orihuela. The castle of Orihuela was besieged and finally taken by the Northmen who used it as a military base over the winter period to strike inland and launch raids on the Balearic Islands.

The ancient Roman arena of Nîmes

In the spring the raiders left the craggy outcrop of Orihuela and sailed off to the Southern coastline of Mediterranean Frankia. The wine producing region of Languedoc Roussilon was the next area to face the fury of the Northmen. The Old Roman towns of Nimes and Arles were attacked and for many of the Scandinavians it would have been the first time that they would have seen the monumental stone buildings such as the Maison Carrée and the Arènes de Nîmes (Roman amphitheatre) relics from a former time of imperial Roman splendor. Over-wintering in the Camague marshlands of the Rhone delta, the Vikings launched raids deep up the Rhone river as far as Valence.

BJÖRN "Ironside"

The following spring the fleet set sail and attacked the coast of Italy. Pisa was razed to the ground and upon hearing that the greatest city in the world 'Rome' was not far away Bjorn and Hastein decided to attack the Eternal city. Mistaking Luna, now Lucca (some 350 kms from the capital) for Rome the Vikings immediately besieged it, but were unable to overcome its formidable defences. As the siege dragged on Bjorn and Hastein hatched a cunning plan to gain entrance into Luna. Bjorn let it be known that he had died, but had converted to Christianity on his deathbed and wished to be buried in consecrated ground inside the city. Eager to have the body interned in the city out of hope of future patronage and pilgrims, the leading burgers of Luna agreed. The unarmed Viking pall bearers carried the coffin along the procession route and upon reaching the city's gates they jammed the entrance open using it. At this very moment the supposedly dead leader Bjorn burst out of the coffin very much alive and handed his compatriots weapons hidden alongside him. Bjorn's men overwhelmed the guards protecting the entrance to the city and let the whole Viking army inside.

After sacking Luna, the raiding fleet headed back towards the straights of Gibraltar, but the element of surprise had now been completely lost. Since the previous raid, the Moorish Principalities had positioned their fleet in the vicinity of Gibraltar to check any further raiding. As Bjorn and Hastein's dragon headed ships rounded the Rock of Gibraltar they were confronted by Moorish warships blockading the straights near Cadiz. Although outnumbered the Vikings were just as well at home fighting on the sea as they were on the land and Bjorn ordered his men to prepare for battle. In the combat several Viking long ships were destroyed, but the majority of the fleet managed to break through the blockade into the Atlantic Ocean.

As Bjorn and Hastein headed north they decided on one last incursion into the heartland of Spain. In a daring attack they infiltrated the Basque Kingdom of Pamplona and captured King García Íñiguez I in the Royal city of Pamplona. The King was threatened with his life and forced to hand over his son and heir as a hostage while he raised a ransom of 70,000 gold dinars.

Pamplona is situated 50 kms from the sea and the strategic position of the Kingdom sandwiched between the Frankish Kingdom to the north, the Moorish Emirate to the south and the Asturias Kingdom to the west made Pamplona a dangerous place to stay too long, with this in mind Bjorn gathered up the ransom money and returned back to his ships. On returning back to the island of Noirmoutier the fleet disbanded. The raid in the south had been one of the greatest adventures of the Viking age and the exploits of Bjorn and Hastein were pasted down to generation after generation.

Hastein "The most wicked of all the Pagans"

Norman Chronicler Dudo of St Quentin on Hastein:

"This was a man accursed: fierce, mightily cruel, and savage, pestilent, hostile, sombre, truculent, given to outrage, pestilent and untrustworthy, fickle and lawless. Death-dealing, uncouth, fertile in ruses, warmonger general, traitor, fomenter of evil, and double-dyeded dissimulator..."

While Bjorn returned to Scandinavia to avenge the death of his father (Ragnar Lodbrok) at the hands of the Northumbrian King Ælla, Hastein took command of the Loire Vikings and planned a new series of raids on the Western Empire. A relative period of calm had descended on Frankia after the Viking warlord Weland had converted to Christianity, allowing King Charles to construct a series of fortifications along the Seine to halt any further Viking incursions. Near Pitres at Pont de l'Arche where the River Seine converges with the River Eure Charles built a fortified bridge with two wooden and stone towers at each end. The King appointed Count Adalhard with the defence of the Seine and Count Robert "the Strong" of Neustria with protecting the Western March against the Bretons and Loire Vikings.

Frankish annals:

"King Charles made all the leaders of his Kingdom meet at a place called Pitres. Where on the one side of the Andelle and on the other side the Eure, flow together into the Seine. They came in June with many carts and began constructing fortifications on the Seine, blocking off the entry of ships going up or down the river because of the Northmen".

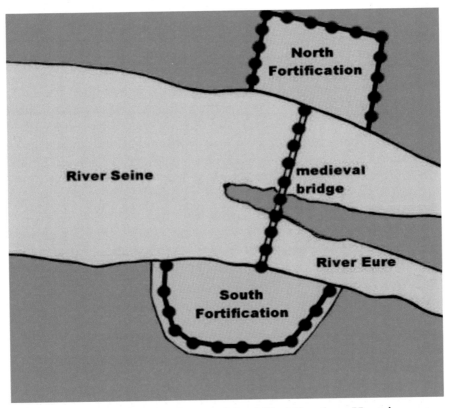

The peace was abruptly shattered in 863 AD when Hastein sent a raiding party up the Loire River. The raiders captured Poitiers, burning down the church of St Hilary. From there they continued inland and according to Archbishop Hincmar de Reims they attacked Clermont, and slew Stephen, son of Count Hugh, returning back to their ships unmolested. This audacious attack was the start of a new phase in the attacks on Western Frankia. With Charles' fortification of the Seine and the murder of the converted Viking warlord Weland in a duel, Hastein moved the focus of Viking activity to the Loire. By doing this he was able to exploit the precarious relationship between the Bretons, Franks and Aquitianians. In 864 AD a more serious development occurred in the south when the former King of Aquitaine Pippin II escaped from sanctuary and went into league with Hastein. Pippin was certainly hoping to regain the Aquitianian crown and be Hastein's puppet King in Bordeaux. His escape was however short lived when he was tricked and captured by some Aquitianians loyal to King Charles. In a show case trial he was brought before the King and accused of renouncing the Christian faith. For this unholy crime and traitorous behaviour he was commended to death. Stripped of his ally in the south, Hastein launched a two pronged attack on Neustria in 865 AD. The main fleet was again sent up the Loire in the direction of Orleans, while a fleet of 50 ships was sent to test the defences of the Seine. The Loire raiders got as far a Fleury and burned Orleans to the ground, apart from the church of the holy cross which resisted their attempts to defile it. When the fleet returned to Noirmoutier with the treasures from the raid Hastein sent out another contingent to attack Poitiers. The city was ransacked in the usual manner, but on their return journey the raiders were ambushed by the forces of Robert "the Strong". Unable to form a shield wall they were cut down and annihilated by Robert's Frankish cavalry. Over 500 Vikings were slaughtered in the encounter. Robert sent a great haul of captured Viking banners and weapons back to Charles as a token of his victory.

Blocked by the fortifications at Pont de l'Arche the Seine Vikings marched on foot to launch an attack on the wine yards of the Vexin region near Paris. This 200 strong force may have even carried a few ships overland using a rolling log system, then re-launching them back into the Seine upstream. The raid proved fruitless and the Vikings returned back to the main force at Oissel Island. Overconfident 500 of them decided to march of foot towards Chartres, but just like at Poitiers they were ambushed and wiped out by a Frankish defence force with only a few survivors managing to get back to their ships on the Seine.

Although both raiding party's had suffered defeats, Hastein had already decided to turn his attention towards Brittany. He had played off one side against the other (Franks and Bretons) during a dispute in 863 AD and now threatened to unleash his entire pagan army upon Brittany. Duke Solaman proposed an agreement in which he would join Hastein in a joint attack on Neustria. Together they marched over the Breton border into Frankia and sacked Le Mans. While the Vikings and Bretons ravaged Anjou, Hastein sent another force south under Sigfried to attack the Frankish controlled areas of Aquitaine. According to the annals of St Bertin this force was defeated with at least 400 causalities and forced to retreat back to the their ships stationed on the River Charente.

At the end of the summer of 865 AD Hastein and Duke Solaman returned to Brittany. King Charles was unable to launch a campaign against the Loire Vikings and Duke Solaman because a new Viking fleet had entered the Seine and had sacked St Denis close to Paris. He was fortunate that this force seems to have contracted some sort of plague, reducing its ability to continue raiding.

Annals of St Bertin

"The Northmen who had sacked St-Denis became ill with various ailments. Some went mad, some were covered in sores, and some discharged their guts with a watery flow through their arses: and so they died."

866 AD: Invasion and the Battle of Brissarthe

On the 29th of December Hastein launched a winter attack into Neustria, but this time they were met by the Frankish forces of Count Gauefrid, Harvey and Rorgo and forced to retreat back to Nantes empty handed. With Hastein's Viking hemmed up in the Loire estuary Charles tasked Robert "the Strong" and his son Odo with clearing out the Seine Vikings who were raiding around Melun. Just as in 845 AD against Ragnar, the Franks divided their forces on either side of the river bank, which led to disastrous consequences. The King watched on helplessly as the Vikings concentrated their attack on Count Robert and Odo's forces. Spearheaded by pagan berserkers, the Vikings pushed the Frankish forces back until Robert ordered his men to retreat before the slaughter became too great. King Charles had no choice but to pay off the raiders with the "Danegeld". The price was high and the King had to raise the taxes all over the Kingdom to pay the 4000 pounds of silver demanded. It was also agreed to pay the Vikings the "wergeld" (compensation for the slain Vikings). The harsh terms for peace did not stop there as any slaves that had escaped from the Northmen were handed back. As a result the Northmen kept their word and sailed back down the Seine to Oissel Island and then Saint Wandrille to repair their ships using timber from the Brotonne forest. Charles immediately marched to Pitres to repair the fortifications over the Seine, hoping to stop any further raiding around Paris.

Abbey of St Wandrille / Fontenelle, Normandy, France

Reinforced by some of the raiders from the Seine, Hastein again in collaboration with Duke Saloman sacked Le Mans in the summer of 866 AD with a mounted force of some 400 men. Robert "the Strong" was determined to destroy this force for once and for all. He was joined by Ranulf I Count of Poitiers, Gauzfrid and Hervey of Maine. On the 15th of September 866 AD the Frankish army managed to cut off Hastein's retreat at Brissarthe. Unable to escape Hastein fortified the church and barricaded himself in, waiting for the Frankish attack. Robert ordered his men to build mounds for siege engines and a wooden palisade to stop the Vikings and Bretons from escaping. From the church bell tower Hastein watched the Frankish movements and realised that he would be trapped unless he moved quickly. Under the cover of darkness he and his men made a break for freedom, but were discovered by the Frankish sentries. Battle was joined and Robert led a cavalry charge straight into the hastily formed Viking shield wall. Hacking his way deep though the Viking ranks, Robert was finally struck down in the thickest of the press and killed. Fighting by his side was Ranulf of Poitiers, who was wounded by a Viking arrow and later died from his injuries.

With the loss of their leaders the Franks called off the attack and retreated. It was a great victory for the Vikings and Bretons who had managed to wipe out the Frankish leadership in the west in one fatal encounter. The situation was so dangerous that Bishop Actard of Nantes even requested a transfer of his post to a safer see.

Surrender at Angers 872 AD

Over the next few years the pattern repeated itself, but Viking military resources may have been diverted to England where the Ragnarsson brothers were piece by piece dismantling the Anglo-Saxon Kingdoms. In 872 AD Hastein was strong enough to launch a daring attack on the Frankish city of Angers. The Vikings stormed the city, plundered it in the fashion of the day, but then dug themselves in. Hastein may have wanted to use Angers as a forward base to launch further attacks on Le Mans, Tours and Laval.

The medieval castle of Angers

The occupation of Angers was a worrying development for King Charles II who risked losing all control and authority over Western Frankia for as long as the city remained in Viking hands. He summoned all the lords of the Kingdom to join him in a campaign to drive Hastein's Vikings from Anjou. King Charles surrounded the city and erected a large earthwork to stop the Vikings from attempting a landward sortie as they had done at Brissarthe. Duke Saloman even joined the Royal host, stationing his men on the other side of the River Mayenne, thus block any escape route to the west. The only way in and out of the city was via the River Maine which the Vikings controlled. Charles was unable to build fortified bridges over the Maine as he had done on the Seine due to the unsuitable terrain. The King's engineers came up with an elaborate plan to divert the river and beach the Viking longships in the muddy waters of the Maine, enabling them useless. After serval abortive attempts to break into Angers Charles agreed and let his engineers put their secret plan into action. Upstream out of the view of Viking eyes the engineers dug a huge canal which succeeded instantly in diverting the course of the river. Not long afterwards the river level dropped leaving the Viking longships high and dry. With no escape Hastein and his men were forced to surrender. In victory King Charles was extremely lenient towards the raiders. After handing over a number of hostages and swearing oaths that they would not attack Charles' Kingdom again they were allowed to return to their island base near Nantes. The King even allowed Hastein to hold a market there and some of his men were even baptised into the Christian faith. Hastein keep his word and did not attack the Frankish Kingdom until after the death of King Charles II "the Bald" in 877 AD

The Siege of Paris 885 AD

Western Frankia suffered a series of short reigning Kings after the death of Charles II "the Bald". This along with an exodus of Viking mercenaries pushed out of Southern England by the resurgent Anglo-Saxons under King Alfred forced many of the raiders to turn their attention towards the continent. In the Low Countries the Vikings suffered two heavy defeats by the Franks at Thimeon (880 AD) and Saucourt (881 AD). Under pressure the leading Viking warlords regrouped and headed south into the Seine estuary for an attack on Paris. According to the Benedictine monk (Abbo de St Germain des Prés) a huge Viking fleet snaked its way up the river Seine towards the capital. Although Abbo was exaggerating the size of the numbers, it was clearly the biggest Viking fleet to attack Western Frankia in living memory.

Abbo de St Germain des Prés

"In the summer of 885 AD seven hundred high-prowed longships and many smaller ones snaked up the River Seine in a column that stretched for more than two leagues (10 kms). The "Grim ones" (Vikings) who rowed those ships were 40,000 thousand strong"

Sigfred, Hastein and possibly Hrolf "the Ganger" the nominally leaders of the raiding fleet offered to spare Paris if the city's defenders allowed them safe passage past the fortified bridges over the Seine, but Odo (Robert 'the Strong's son), Goslin (Bishop of Paris) refused and prepared the city for the Viking onslaught. Paris was still an island citadel and only had two bridges that connected it to either side of the River Seine. In order to capture the city Sigfred had to take one of these two bridges. On the morning of the 26th of November 885 AD the Vikings launched an assault on the northern bridge. The fighting was ferocious, as the pagans tried to scale to defensive tower, using makeshift ladders and grappling hooks. Intern the Parisians poured burning pitch and hot oil onto them below. By nightfall the Vikings withdrew with heavy losses.

19th century depiction of the siege of Paris 885 AD

During the night Count Odo's men repaired the tower and even added another wooden story from which they could wreak havoc upon the Vikings if they dared attack again.

On the second day of the siege the Vikings came again, this time using a battering ram to try and force their way in. The battle raged on all day until nightfall when the Vikings broke off the attack and retreated back to their camp at the Abbey of St Germain l'Auxerois. After two unsuccessful attempts resulting in heavy casualties Sigfred decided to surround the city and try and starve the garrison into submission.

After two months of investing the city the Vikings believed that the defenders were weak enough to try another attack. On the 31st of January 886 AD they attacked both bridges simultaneously. For the next three days the Parisians fought desperately to stop Sigfred's men from entering Paris. The Vikings tried to gain closer access to the northern tower by filling in the moat around it with everything available, including the bodies of the dead. Three fire ships were also sent up the River Seine, crashing into the bank below the tower. In early February severe floods hit the region, as the water level rose the southern bridge was washed away, leaving the tower cut off from the island citadel. Unable to flee, the defenders fought on until the tower was finally destroyed by the Vikings. Now with a way to bypass Paris, part of the Viking fleet sailed on and ravaged the surrounding region, launching raids as far off as Chartres, Le Mans and Evreux. Bishop Goslin sent urgent riders to the Emperor who was campaigning in Italy requesting help. When news reached Vikings ears that the Emperor was returning and that Henry of Saxony's troops were marching towards Paris, Sigfred and the Viking leaders ordered their men to regroup on the safer left bank of the Seine. During early spring of 886 AD no help came for the beleaguered defenders and the situation became desperate when the charismatic Bishop Goslin died. Count Odo took over sole command and secretly left the city to get help from the Emperor personally.

His mission was successful and Charles III "the Fat" sent him back to Paris with an armed escort. Fighting his way through the Norse lines Odo re-entered the city with fresh hope for the defenders. Sigfred decided on one last attempt to break into Paris. The Vikings attacked, but were beaten back by the rejuvenated Parisians. In October the imperial forces relived the city and invested the Viking encampment on the River Seine. Instead of finally crushing the Viking menace, the Emperor entered into negotiations and recruited many of them to act as mercenaries against rebel Frankish lords in Burgundy possibly including Hrolf "the Ganger".

Count Odo was disgusted by the treaty and blocked off the Seine to Sigfred's men, forcing them to haul their long ships overland in order to bypass Paris. The capital had been saved, but the Seine estuary had been all but abandoned to the Vikings who over wintered there every year and even started to colonise and create new settlements. In 888 AD the Emperor Charles was deposed and the Western Franks elected the hero of the siege of Paris, Count Odo as their new King. Odo was determined to rid the Kingdom of the Vikings once and for all. In a campaign against the Northmen in Burgundy he surprised a raiding party near Verdun and although outnumbered he defeated them at the Battle of Montfaucon. In the spring of 889 AD another force of Vikings captured Meaux and threatened to besiege Paris again. Odo this time bought off the Northmen with the 'Danegeld'. The raiders left and attacked

Western Neustria, sacking St Lo, but were themselves annihilated by a combined force of Franks and Bretons in the thick wooded valleys of the Cotentin.

The old warlord Hastein had settled the Somme valley after the siege of Paris, but with the resurgent Franks attacking his frontier settlements he decided to quit the continent forever and embark on one last adventure. This time his objective was to conquer the Kingdom of Wessex (England).

19th century depiction of Hastein

Taking command of the remnants of the "Great Heathen Army" Hastein tried to replicate the earlier invasion of the Ragnarsson brothers, but Wessex had learnt the lessons from over 14 years of brutal warfare against the Northmen and defeated his army in several skirmishes and battles. In 893 AD Hastein disappeared from the annals of history, probably killed when the Anglo-Saxons overran his long port at Benfleet in Essex or in the battle of Buttington on the English Welsh border near Welshpool.

Hastein

The last campaign in Brittany

With the departure of Hastein, Hrolf "the Ganger" emerged as leader of the Seine Vikings. In 911 AD after a partial defeat by the Franks at Chartres Hrolf agreed to meet with the new King, Charles III "the Simple". Charles offered Hrolf the land from the River Epte to the sea, if he and his followers became Christian and stopped any further Viking incursions into Neustria. Hrolf agreed and became the King's man in the newly created Duchy of Normandy (See my book, THE SEAWOLVES "The Viking creation of Normandy") With Normandy, especially the Seine valley now closed off from any raiding the only option for newly arrived war bands was to either give up the sword for the plough in Normandy or sail on and try their luck by attacking the independent Kingdom of Brittany further west.

Brittany had been relatively free from any major Viking attacks since the Breton King Alan I "the Great" had driven them out in 892 AD after the battles of Questembert and St Lo. The death of Alan in 907 AD coincided with the Viking establishment of the Duchy of Normandy and for the Vikings who were not prepared to settle down, only Brittany and Ireland offered the best success for raiding. As early as 912 AD Viking attacks intensified on the Celtic Kingdom. The raiders attacked the usual targets of the richly endowed monasteries, including Saint Guenolé. The situation became so serious that many of the Breton monastic communities were forced to flee across the border into Frankia with their sacred relics and precious manuscripts. In 914 AD the Anglo-Saxon chronicle stated that a large fleet of Danes under the command of Haraldr and Otarr sailed from the Seven estuary to attack Brittany. After ravaging Brittany for several years Haraldr and Otarr set sail to continue their raiding spree elsewhere in the British Isles. If the Bretons hoped for a rest bite they were sadly mistaken, in 919 AD an even bigger Viking fleet appeared off the coastline of the Loire estuary. This fleet was commanded by the Norwegian warlord Rognvaldur. Whether Rognvaldur had received intelligence from the Viking trading network of the political disarray in Brittany or from the Norse colonists in Normandy is unclear, but he was intent on not just raiding Brittany, but outright conquest. Nantes was quickly captured and used as a base from which to overrun the Breton Kingdom.

Viking war bands spread out across the Kingdom and hunted down the Breton aristocracy and clerics who refused to capitulate and offered resistance to their rule. Alan Baretorte /twisted bread (grandson of Alan I) managed to evade his Viking pursuers and took ship to Anglo-Saxon England, where he remained in exile. Within two years the Kingdom had been completely pacified. The Frankish chronicler Flodoard de Reims even mentions the term 'slave raiding'. This comment may refer that Rognvaldur was trying to turn Nantes into a Viking trading hub such as Rouen, Jorvik (York) or Dublin. Nantes was fortified by Rognvaldur's men and withstood a Frankish siege for five months to try and retake the city. Unable to force the Vikings from Nantes, Robert I of Neustria ceded to county over to Rognvaldur, on the condition that he and his men convert to Christianity.

Both Rognvaldur and Hrolf of Normandy were drawn into the Frankish civil war between King Charles III "the Simple" and his nobles. In siding with the King, Rognvaldur may have been hoping to receive a similar settlement as Hrolf had done in 911 AD. If so, he was misled and received nothing from the King. According to Flodoard he went berserk and led a raid deep into Frankia, ravaging Aquitaine and Auvergne. In 925 AD Rognvaldur was confronted by the combined force of Frankish nobles commanded by Hugh the Great (Count of Paris), Herbert of Vermandois and Raoul I near Chalmont. In the ensuing battle Rognvaldur's Vikings were forced into a fighting withdrawal all the way back to Nantes. According to the 'Miracles of St Benedict' the Viking warlord died shortly afterwards. A divine punishment for attacking the Abbey of Fleury, his death was marked by strange apparitions of strange lights in the sky and moving rocks. Hugh the Great's forces followed up their victory by besieging Nantes. After a month of unsuccessfully besieging the city a truce was agreed in which Nantes was again ceded over to the pagans.

In 931 AD Viking contingents from all over Brittany were summoned by their new leader Felekan to convene at Nantes in order to prepare for an all-out assault on Frankia. As the warriors left their protected villages and settlements, the Breton population that had been occupied for nearly 30 years seized their chance and rose up in rebellion. Using guerilla tactics, small parties of Viking soldiers were ambushed and slaughtered including Felekan himself.

Incon a subordinate Viking commander took charge of the occupation force before all was lost and launched a vicious counter attack against the Bretons.

Although he restored order, Viking authority in Brittany had been greatly weakened. The Viking position in Brittany was further threatened when Hrolf's son and heir William I 'Longsword' of Normandy made an alliance with Hugh the Great in 935 AD. This left Incon completely isolated without an ally in the fledgling Viking colony of Normandy. With the Franks fortifying the Breton March and an indigenous population growing more defiant by the day it was only a matter of time before Viking rule in Brittany was challenged.

Cross of Alan II "Barbetorte" Plourivo

The situation came to a head in 936 AD when Alan II "Barbetorte/twisted beard" returned from exile with a contingent of Anglo-Saxon troops supplied by his foster father King Æthelstan of Wessex and embarked on the re-conquest of Brittany. Landing at Dol, Alan began the re-conquest of Brittany in earnest and caught the local Viking occupation force reveling inside the sacred ground of a desecrated monastery. Caught by complete surprise, the Vikings were captured and executed as a show of intent. Alan at once marched west on to the Viking stronghold of Peran near Saint Brieuc. Peasants and nobles alike flocked to his banner, eager to oust the Vikings from the Kingdom. The Viking fort (Camp de Péran) was a huge irregular circular fortress, with 4 meter high walls, some 5 meters thick. Alan needed to destroy this fortress in order to break the Viking grip in Northern Brittany.

The Viking warriors entrenched themselves inside the fortress and were confident of holding out until a relief force could be sent from Nantes. Although Péran had a well and had been stocked full of provisions Alan II had no intention of conducting a lengthy siege. Sensing momentum was on his side; he stormed the fortress and overrun the Viking garrison. The defenders were slaughtered until the last man and Péran was burned to the ground. The symbolic capture of the mighty fortress of Péran forced the Vikings into a full scale retreat, abandoning their settlements they fled towards Nantes.

Aerial view of the Camp de Péran, Brittany, France

Alan swept away the last resistance in the north by destroying another Viking encampment (Castel Affret) at the battle of Plourivo. After his victory over the pagans he erected a stone cross, which can still be seen to this day. The Northmen decided to make a final stand at a fortified position just outside Nantes near Saint Aignan. The Bretons led an assault on the Viking defences, but were beaten back with heavy loses. Undeterred Alan II galvanized his men into making a second attack. The fighting raged on all day in horrendous weather conditions. As the torrential rain soaked both defenders and attackers the ground became boggy and run red with blood from the vicious hand to hand combat. Finally just before dusk the Bretons gained the upper hand the breached the Viking ramparts. As they poured into the Viking encampment the surviving Northmen retreated to the safely of their longships anchored on the banks of the river Loire. Defeated and broken the remaining Vikings sailed away down the Loire estuary as the triumphant Bretons and their savior Alan II entered Nantes.

According to the Chronicle of Nantes he had to cut his way through the thick brambles and weeds that covered the entrance of the city's cathedral, which had being neglected for nearly twenty years.

Plaque commemorating Alain II "Barbetorte" victory over the Vikings, Nantes, France

The remnants of the defeated Viking army regrouped on the Island of Noirmoutier and landed on the Breton mainland again in 939 AD determined to avenge their defeat at Nantes two years earlier. They marched into the heartland of Brittany and fortified themselves inside the fortress of Trans near Rennes. In the summer of 939 AD a joint Breton and Frankish force led by Alan II, Count Bérenger and Hugh "the Great" surrounded the fortress and extinguished the Viking menace forever, killing all the raiders inside and razing the fortress to the ground. Although there was further sporadic raiding, the Viking dream of creating a second Normandy in Brittany was over.

Aquitaine and Galicia, 876-982 AD

The fall of "Viking Brittany" left only a few bastions of pagan influence dotted along the Aquitainian coastline. Frothaire, the Bishop of Bordeaux had abandoned his see in 876 AD, stating that Bordeaux was desolate because of the persecutions of the heathens. In 887 AD the Pope sent Leon de Carentan to Aquitaine the convert the pagans to Christianity. Leon was chosen because he spoke Norse and had lived alongside the Vikings in Normandy. Leon's work was a success and he helped bring many of the permanent Viking settlements into the Christian faith. However when preaching in the furthest reaches of Aquitaine near Bayonne, he was captured by the heathens and decapitated for offending the old gods.

Modern depiction of a Viking warrior, Catoira, Galicia

A large Viking fleet was welcomed by Duke Richard I "the Fearless" of Normandy in 962 AD to fight as mercenaries against an attempted Frankish invasion of the Duchy. Once the campaign was over Duke Richard offered land in return for baptism and service for those who wanted to settle down in the fledgling state. The remainder of the fleet (some 100 longships) left Rouen and sailed south around Brittany and into the Bay of Biscay.

According to the Moorish Chronicler (Ibn Al-Idari) in 966 AD part of the same fleet attacked Lisbon and Alcacer do Sal. Realising the region was too well defended they turned their attention towards Galicia. On receiving reports of Viking activity Bishop Sisnando II at once mustered the local levies into a force to combat the raiders from the north.

'Torres de Oueste' built on the River Ulla to defend Catoira and Santiago de Compostela against Viking attacks. Catoira, Galicia

In 968 AD the fleet regrouped under the command of Gunrod, possibly with reinforcements from Aquitaine and launched a major assault on the Arousa estuary. The fleet of 100 long ships was able to field a force of some 3000-4000 fighting men. The target of this formidable force was the holy town of Santiago de Compostela. A place of pilgrimage dedicated to Saint James, Santiago de Compostela had grown rich since the last major Viking raid of Bjorn "Ironside" and Hastein over 100 years before. In 960 AD Bishop Sisnando II had foreseen just such an attack and had fortified Compostela with a defensive wall and watch towers. The formidable fortress of the 'Torres de Oeste' protecting the River Ulla was strengthened and signal stations were positioned at strategic positions along the coast to forewarn of any danger from the sea. This system paid dividends when the fort of A Lanzanda spotted the Viking fleet as it entered the Arousa estuary and alerted Bishop Sisnando II in Compostela. The Vikings landed near Catoira and plundered the poorly defended settlements along the River Ulla.

The Bishop's army confronted them at a place called Fornelos near the River Louro on the 29th of March and decided to give battle. Gunrod organized his men into a dense shield wall and advanced towards the Bishop's army, flying Odin's raven banner.

The Bishop also rallied his men with Christian zeal and ordered a general attack on the Viking lines. As the two armies interlocked together, axe, sword and spear were used to deadly effect, but it was a Viking arrow that decided the day. At the crucial moment Bishop Sisnando was struck in the face by a stray Viking arrow and killed instantly. As the news of his death spread through the Galician ranks, panic set in and the Christian soldiers broke off the combat and fled in terror. Gunrod was victorious and the Galician defeat at Fornelos left the region virtually undefended.

Santiago de Compostela was ransacked and over the next three years Gunrod's Vikings roamed at will and terrorised the local population. Christian churches were pulled down and no compromise could be reached with the heathens who launched raids deep into the heartland of Galicia.

Reconstructed Viking ships used in the 'Romaría Vikinga' Viking festival, Catoira, Galicia, Spain

Chronicle of Sampiro
"Gunderedo (Gunrod) penetrated the cities of Galicia and caused untold damage around St James de Compostela. Bishop Sisenado succumbed to the sword and all of Galicia was plundered up to the Cebreiro Mountains".

After three whole years of destruction and blood letting the situation finally came to a head when Bishop Rosendo of San Martin de Mondonedo and now Compostela organized a new army under the command of Count Gonzalo Sánchez to crush the invaders for once and for all. After being unchallenged since the Battle of Fornelos Gunrod was caught unprepared and forced to fight the Galicians with only part of his army. This time the Vikings were overwhelmed and annihilated in the battle. Gunrod refused to yield or be captured and fought the Viking way sword in hand until he was cut down in the melee. With their leader lying dead on the field of battle, Viking unity in Galicia crumbled. Many returned to their ships, safely harboured in Viking long ports on the coast and returned home to the North. So ended the Viking dream of creating a Kingdom in the sun. Galicia was raided again in a notable raid by Olaf Haraldsson (later King and Saint Olaf of Norway). Olaf's men sailed up the River Minho and burnt the town of Tui to the ground, capturing Bishop Don Alfonso in the process. But this was just a mere raid for plunder rather than any attempt to secure land for a new colony. Recent archaeological excavations on the Galician coastline have revealed a fortified settlement near O Vicedo in the province of Lugo. Two stone anchors were found at the site, possibly used by large Viking long ships. It is possible that this site amongst others were settled by Gunrod's followers who may have stayed behind and converted to Christianity.

The rich pilgrim city of Santiago de Compostela, Galicia, Spain

GUNROD

While Gunrod's force was in Galicia, the Aquitainians decided the time was right to eradicate the last Viking enclaves in the region. In 970 AD Count William "The Good" of Bordeaux launched a major campaign against the Vikings, but was defeated and then ransomed back to the Franks. During the rest of his reign the two communities lived in relative peace and harmony. It was left to his heir, Count William II Sánchez of Gascony to finally remove the Vikings from Aquitaine in 982 AD. Near Dax at the elusive battle of Taller a confederation of Vikings was finally defeated, leaving the survivors to either convert to Christianity or leave Aquitaine soil forever.

Viking raiders sporadically attacked Frankia, but their attention turned towards the rich Kingdom of Æthelred the Unready's England. The Viking colony of Normandy prospered and in time would pose a headache for the Kings of France, but that is another story in itself.

Conclusion

For nearly 200 years the Sækonungr (Sea Kings) had raided, plundered and colonised large areas of Western continental Europe, from Dorestad in the north to Spain in the south. The raiding of the so called "Great Heathen Army" on the continent although devastatingly destructive also helped to shape the great Fiefdoms of early medieval France, Spain and the dynasties that ruled them. Perhaps their great legacy was the creation of the Duchy of Normandy of which within 150 years of being founded became the most feared Principality in Western Europe.

Also Available:

THE GREAT HEATHEN ARMY
Ivar "the Boneless" and the Viking invasion of Britain"

THE LAST VIKING
King Harald III "Hardrada" the hero of a Thousand battles

Other titles in the series
"The Normans"

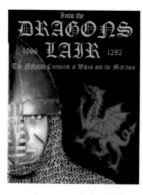

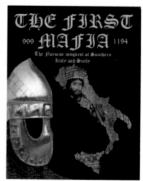

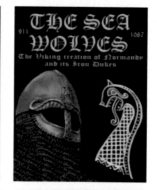

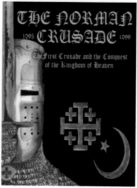
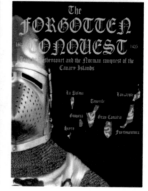

Made in the USA
San Bernardino, CA
11 August 2017